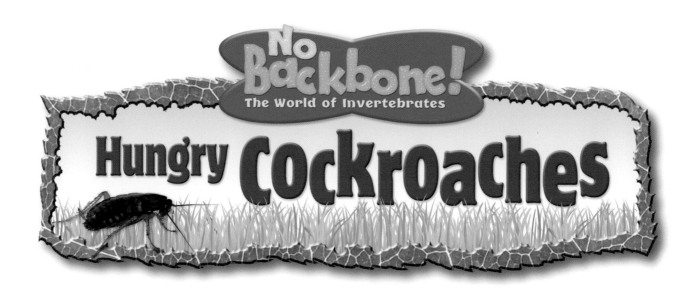

Hungry Cockroaches

No Backbone!
The World of Invertebrates

by Meish Goldish

Consultant: Brian V. Brown
Curator, Entomology Section
Natural History Museum of Los Angeles County

BEARPORT
PUBLISHING

NEW YORK, NEW YORK

Credits

Cover, © Marcus M. Jones/Shutterstock; 4, © NHPA/Ken Griffiths; 5, © Dwight Kuhn/Dwight Kuhn Photography; 6, © Nigel Cattlin/Holt Studios International Ltd/Alamy; 7, © Dwight Kuhn/Dwight Kuhn Photography; 8T, © Stephen Dalton/Minden Pictures; 8C, © Gail M. Shumway/Bruce Coleman; 8B, © Stephen Dalton/Minden Pictures; 9, © Tobias Gremme/DAS FOTOARCHIV/Peter Arnold; 10, © Bates Littlehales/Animals Animals-Earth Scenes; 11, © Jim Mires/Alamy; 12, © Bryan Lowry/Seapics.com; 13, © Emanuele Biggi/Oxford Scientific Films/Photolibrary; 15, © Pat Morris/Ardea; 16T, © Kim Taylor/npl/Minden Pictures; 16B, © Gilbert S. Grant/Photo Researchers, Inc.; 17, © Heidi & Hans-Jurgen Koch/animal-affairs.com/Digital Railroad; 18, © Patti Murray/Animals Animals-Earth Scenes; 19, © Heidi & Hans-Jurgen Koch/animal-affairs.com/Digital Railroad; 20, © Tobias Gremme/DAS FOTOARCHIV/Peter Arnold; 21, © Susan Van Etten/PhotoEdit; 22TL, © Don Klein/SuperStock; 22TR, © Piotr Naskrecki/Minden Pictures; 22BL, © Creatas/SuperStock; 22BR, © age fotostock/SuperStock; 23TL, © Jim Wehtje/Photodisc Green/Getty Images; 23TR, © Kim Taylor/npl/Minden Pictures; 23BL, © Nigel Cattlin/Holt Studios International Ltd/Alamy; 23BR, © Heidi & Hans-Jurgen Koch/animal-affairs.com/Digital Railroad.

Publisher: Kenn Goin
Editorial Director: Adam Siegel
Creative Director: Spencer Brinker
Design: Dawn Beard Creative
Photo Researcher: Nancy Tobin

Library of Congress Cataloging-in-Publication Data

Goldish, Meish.
  Hungry cockroaches / by Meish Goldish.
     p. cm. — (No backbone! The world of invertebrates series)
  Includes bibliographical references and index.
  ISBN-13: 978-1-59716-588-4 (library binding)
  ISBN-10: 1-59716-588-3 (library binding)
  1. Cockroaches—Juvenile literature. I. Title.

QL505.5.G65 2008
595.7'28—dc22
                              2007039188

For more information, write to Bearport Publishing Company, Inc., 101 Fifth Avenue, Suite 6R, New York, New York 10003. Printed in the United States of America.

10 9 8 7 6 5 4 3 2 1

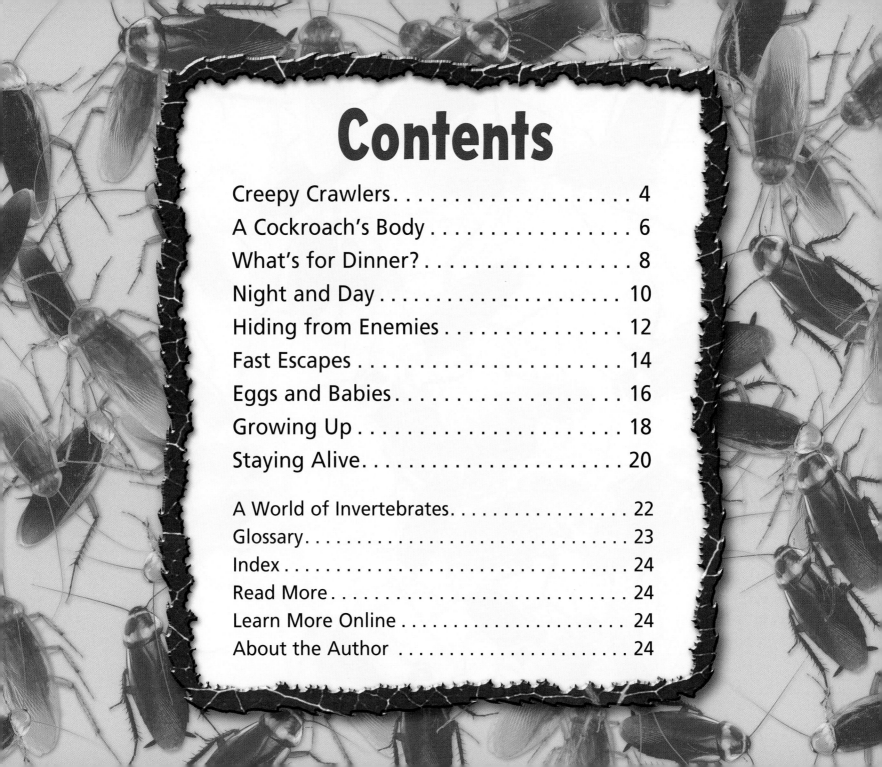

Contents

Creepy Crawlers. 4

A Cockroach's Body 6

What's for Dinner? 8

Night and Day 10

Hiding from Enemies 12

Fast Escapes 14

Eggs and Babies. 16

Growing Up 18

Staying Alive. 20

A World of Invertebrates. 22

Glossary. 23

Index 24

Read More 24

Learn More Online 24

About the Author 24

Creepy Crawlers

Cockroaches are **insects** that come out at night to find food.

People think of them as pests that crawl and spread germs in their kitchens.

Yet most cockroaches don't live in houses and apartments.

They live in the wild, far from people's homes.

There are more than 3,500 kinds of cockroaches all over the world. Most live in warm, wet places like rain forests.

5

A Cockroach's Body

Like all insects, a cockroach has six legs and two antennas.

Its strong legs help it run fast.

The antennas look like two long, wiggling hairs.

The roach uses them to feel and smell food.

antennas

legs

Cockroaches and all
other insects have
a hard covering called an
exoskeleton. The exoskeleton
protects the soft inner parts
of an insect's body.

What's for Dinner?

Cockroaches will eat almost anything.

Bread crumbs, meat, fruit, potatoes, and candy all taste good to them.

Cockroaches also eat wood, paper, soap, paint, and glue.

In the wild, they eat plants and dead animals.

They must also drink water, or they will dry out and die.

Cockroaches walk in garbage and rotting food as they eat. They then spread germs when they move around a house.

9

Night and Day

Cockroaches try to stay away from any light.

They wait until night to come out and eat.

During the day, they rest in dark places.

Cockroaches will not hunt for food in daylight, even if they are very hungry.

Cockroaches in a dark kitchen or bathroom will scurry away quickly if someone turns on a light.

11

Hiding from Enemies

Cockroaches have many enemies in the wild.

Snakes, mice, lizards, and birds are just a few of the animals that eat them.

Spiders and insects feed on them, too.

By staying in the dark, roaches are often able to hide from their enemies.

spider

cockroach

Some cockroaches give off a bad smell that keeps enemies away.

Fast Escapes

Cockroaches find out quickly when danger is on the way.

Tiny hairs on their bodies can feel the air move, even just a little.

If they sense trouble, the roaches scoot away.

Their strong legs make them one of the fastest-running insects.

Their flat bodies can slip quickly into small holes and cracks.

Most cockroaches have wings, but they don't fly from enemies. They usually run away instead.

Eggs and Babies

Female cockroaches make an **egg case** with their bodies.

Then they lay their eggs in the case and leave it somewhere safe.

When the eggs inside hatch, the babies swallow lots of air.

They get so big that the egg case splits open.

Baby cockroaches, called **nymphs**, crawl out of the case.

egg case

egg cases

nymphs

Cockroach nymphs
look like adults, only
smaller. They are born
white, but they turn
black or brown as
they grow.

17

Growing Up

Cockroach nymphs are born with exoskeletons.

The young insects grow until these coverings become too tight and split open.

Then they crawl out of their old exoskeletons and form new ones.

This change is called molting.

Most cockroaches molt 6 to 13 times before they become adults.

Adult cockroaches usually live from six months to five years.

old exoskeleton

nymph

18

Staying Alive

Many people try to kill cockroaches in their homes.

They set out poison, or they try to step on them.

Yet roaches are often too fast or too tricky for people.

They can use their senses to tell if a food is poison and then stay away from it.

Cockroaches have lived on Earth a long time, and they will most likely survive for a long time to come.

Roaches have been around for more than 300 million years. They were living on Earth even before the time of the dinosaurs.

A World of Invertebrates

An animal that has a skeleton with a **backbone** inside its body is a *vertebrate* (VUR-tuh-brit). Mammals, birds, fish, reptiles, and amphibians are all vertebrates.

An animal that does not have a skeleton with a backbone inside its body is an *invertebrate* (in-VUR-tuh-brit). More than 95 percent of all kinds of animals on Earth are invertebrates.

Some invertebrates, such as insects and spiders, have hard skeletons—called exoskeletons—on the outside of their bodies. Other invertebrates, such as worms and jellyfish, have soft, squishy bodies with no exoskeletons to protect them.

Here are four insects that are closely related to cockroaches. Like all insects, they are invertebrates.

Grasshopper

Katydid

Cricket

Earwig

Glossary

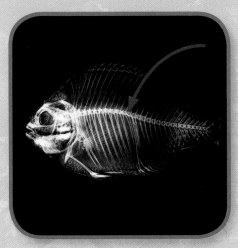

backbone
(BAK-*bohn*)
a group of connected bones that run along the backs of some animals, such as dogs, cats, and fish; also called a spine

egg case
(EG KAYSS)
the container that a female cockroach makes to protect her eggs until they hatch

insects (IN-sekts)
small animals that have six legs, three main body parts, two antennas, and a hard covering called an exoskeleton

nymphs (NIMFS)
young insects that change into adults by growing and shedding their exoskeleton again and again

Index

antennas 6

backbone 22

cricket 22

earwig 22

eggs 16

enemies 12–13, 14, 20

exoskeleton 7, 18–19, 22

food 4, 6, 8–9, 10, 20

germs 4, 9

grasshopper 22

katydid 22

legs 6, 14

life cycle 16–17, 18–19

molting 18–19

nighttime 4, 10

nymphs 16–17, 18

wings 14

Read More

Brimner, Larry Dane. *Cockroaches.* Danbury, CT: Children's Press (1999).

Green, Emily K. *Cockroaches.* Minneapolis, MN: Bellwether Media (2006).

Learn More Online

To learn more about cockroaches, visit

www.bearportpublishing.com/NoBackbone-Insects

About the Author

Meish Goldish has written more than 100 books for children. He lives in Brooklyn, New York.